Garbage

Alan Trussell-Cullen

Australia • Brazil • Japan • Korea • Mexico • Singapore • Spain • United Kingdom • United States

Garbage

Fast Forward
Purple Level 19

Text: Alan Trussell-Cullen
Illustrations: Mark Wilson
Editor: Cameron Macintosh
Designer: James Lowe
Series designer: James Lowe
Production controller: Seona Galbally
Photo research: Fiona Smith
Audio recordings: Juliet Hill, Picture Start
Spoken by: Matthew King and Abbe Holmes
Reprint: Siew Han Ong

Acknowledgements
The author and publisher would like to acknowledge permission to reproduce material from the following sources: Photographs by Alamy/ alwaystock, LLC/ Don Spiro, p. 16; Alamy/ David Hoffman Photo Library, pp. 18, 19; Alamy/ Woodfall Wild Images/ David Woodfall, p. 15; iStockphoto.com, p. 20; iStockphoto.com/ Alister Jupp, p. 3; iStockphoto.com/ David Freund, p. 5; iStockphoto.com/ Joy Fera, front cover; iStockphoto.com/ Tim Dalek, p. 22 centre; Newsphotos/ Mark Frecker, p. 23; Newspix/ Gregg Porteous, p. 21; Photolibrary.com/ Index Stock Imagery/ Photo Communications Inc Omni, p. 6; Photolibrary/ Alamy/ Alex Segre, p. 13; Photolibrary/ Alamy/ Barry Mason, p. 22 bottom; Photolibrary/ Alamy/ Jack Sullivan, p. 7 left; Photolibrary/ Alamy/ Paul Doyle, p. 11; Photolibrary/ Alamy/ Robert Brook, p. 10; Photolibrary/ Alamy/ The Photolibrary Wales, p. 8; Photolibrary/ Oxford Scientific Films/ Tony Tilford, p. 9; Photolibrary/ Science Photo Library, p. 12; Photolibrary/ Science Photo Library/ Robert Brook, pp. 4, 7 right; Photolibrary/ Science Photo Library/ Simon Fraser, p. 14.

ISBN 978 0 17 012650 2
ISBN 978 0 17 012645 8 (set)

Cengage Learning Australia
Level 7, 80 Dorcas Street
South Melbourne, Victoria Australia 3205
Phone: 1300 790 853

Cengage Learning New Zealand
Unit 4B Rosedale Office Park
331 Rosedale Road, Albany, North Shore NZ 0632
Phone: 0800 449 725

For learning solutions, visit **cengage.com.au**

Printed in Australia by Ligare Pty Ltd
8 9 10 11 12 13 14 22 21 20 19 18

THE UNIVERSITY OF MELBOURNE

Evaluated in independent research by staff from the Department of Language, Literacy and Arts Education at the University of Melbourne.

GARBAGE

Alan Trussell-Cullen

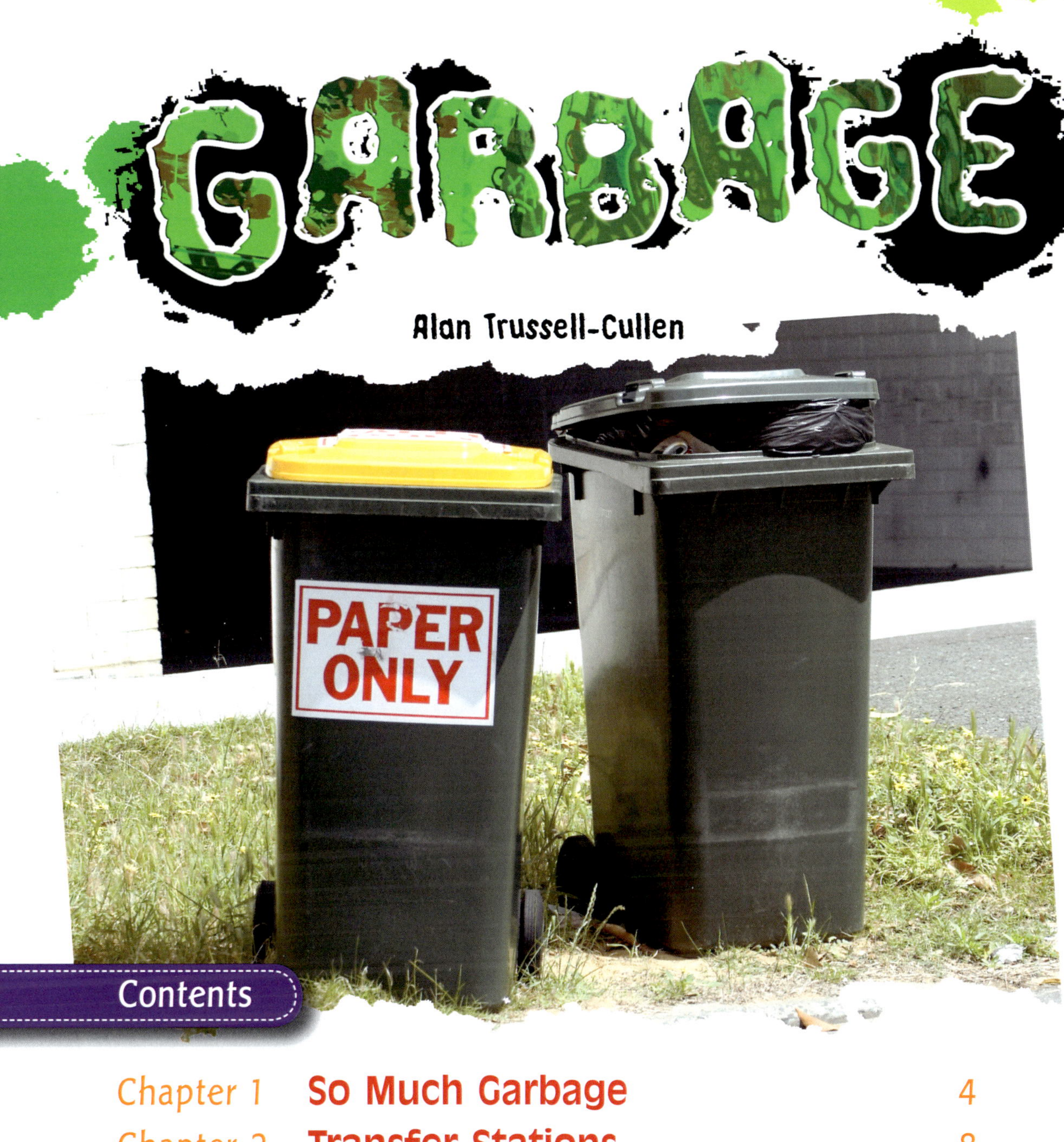

Contents

Chapter 1

SO MUCH GARBAGE

Garbage is the name given to all the things people throw away.
Other names for garbage are trash, rubbish and waste.

People create a lot of garbage.
In Australia, people send about a tonne of garbage per person a year to **landfill**.
That's nearly three kilograms per person, every day of the year.

Garbage comes from people's homes, offices and schools.
It also comes from factories and farms.

The problem with garbage is finding the best way to get rid of it.

In most big cities, garbage is collected at the kerb in trucks and taken to transfer stations.

From here, it may be sent to an incinerator to be burnt, or it may be recycled or sent to a landfill.

Garbage is burnt in incinerators at high temperatures. One problem with burning garbage is that the smoke may contain harmful chemicals that pollute the air.

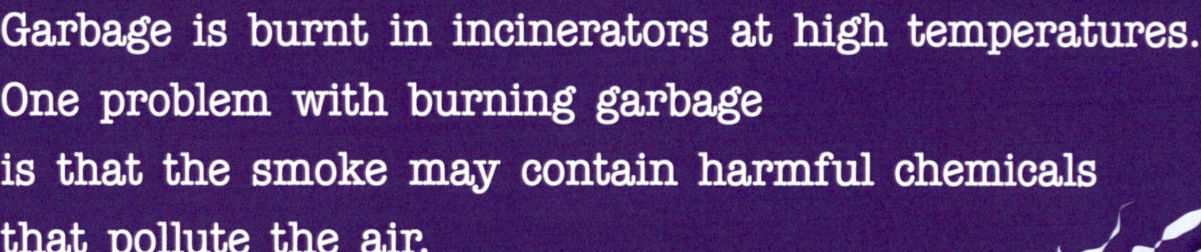

A lot of the garbage collected can be recycled. More and more garbage is being recycled, but most garbage still ends up as landfill.

Chapter 2

TRANSFER STATIONS

In the past, people dumped their garbage in garbage dumps and landfills near the cities and towns where they lived. Most of these old town dumps or landfills weren't well looked after.

They attracted rats and flies,
and everything got dumped together,
which meant harmful chemicals leaked out
and poisoned the **ground water**.

Today, land close to a city is too valuable to use for dumping garbage. Now, garbage is taken great distances to more suitable places.

First, however, garbage collected off the kerb
is taken to a transfer station.
Here, the garbage is sorted,
and people decide what to do with it.

Some garbage may be recycled, but any dangerous garbage is sent to a suitable **toxic waste dump**.

toxic waste dump

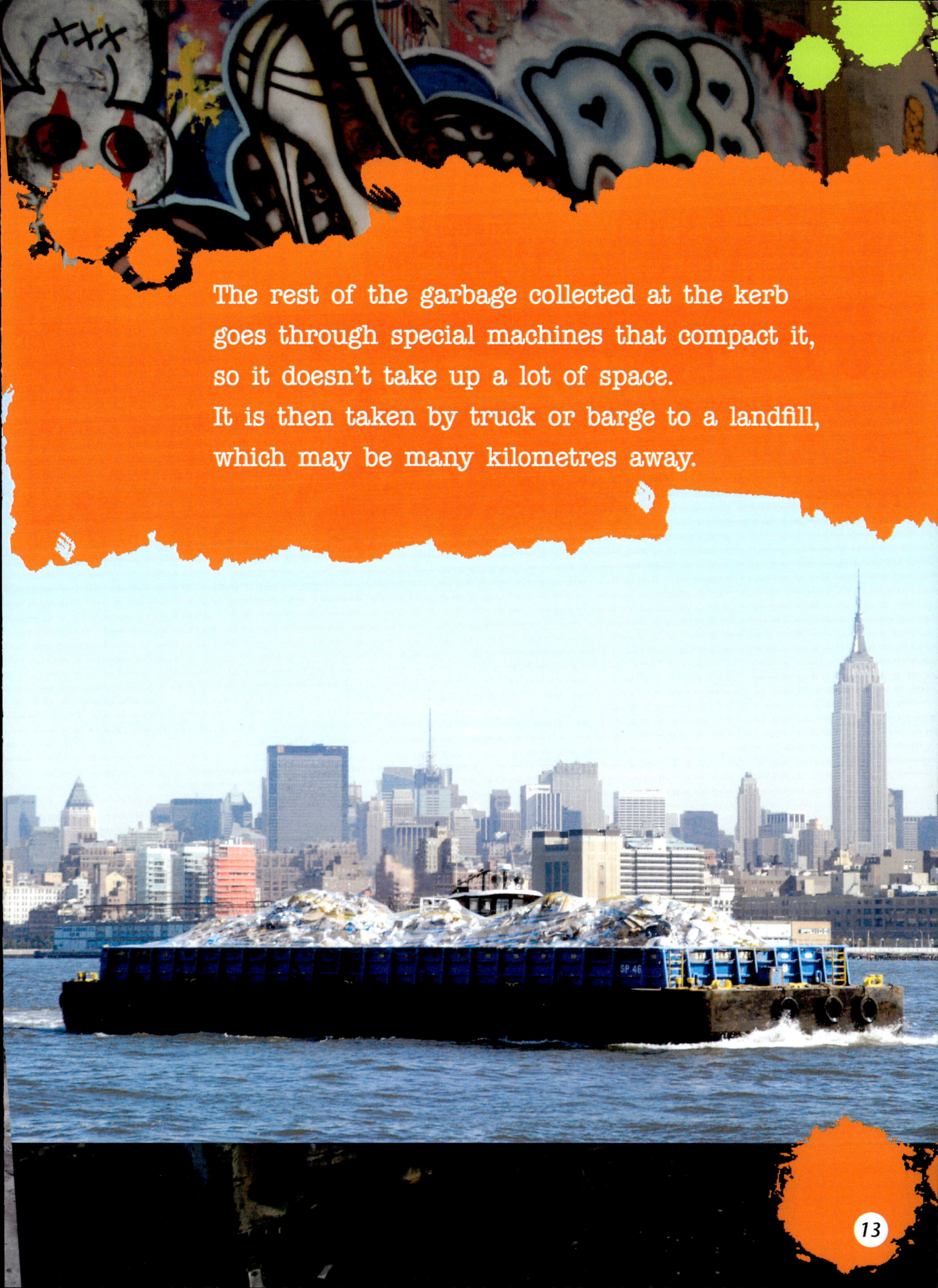

The rest of the garbage collected at the kerb goes through special machines that compact it, so it doesn't take up a lot of space.
It is then taken by truck or barge to a landfill, which may be many kilometres away.

Chapter 3

LANDFILLS

A landfill is a large piece of land that has been set aside for dumping garbage.

A modern landfill is specially built
to store garbage safely.
It is usually lined with plastic to make sure
that any harmful chemicals left in the garbage
don't pollute the ground water.

Large landfills may take garbage
from many towns and cities,
and sometimes even from other countries.

As sections of the landfill become full,
they are covered over and sealed tightly.

As the garbage inside breaks down,
it gives off gases.
Sometimes, people at landfills collect the gases
given off by garbage.
The gases can be used to make electricity.

Chapter 4

TOXIC WASTE DUMPS

Garbage from some factories may contain dangerous chemicals that cannot be dumped in an ordinary landfill. Some of this garbage is burnt in incinerators, but most of it gets placed in special landfills called toxic waste dumps.

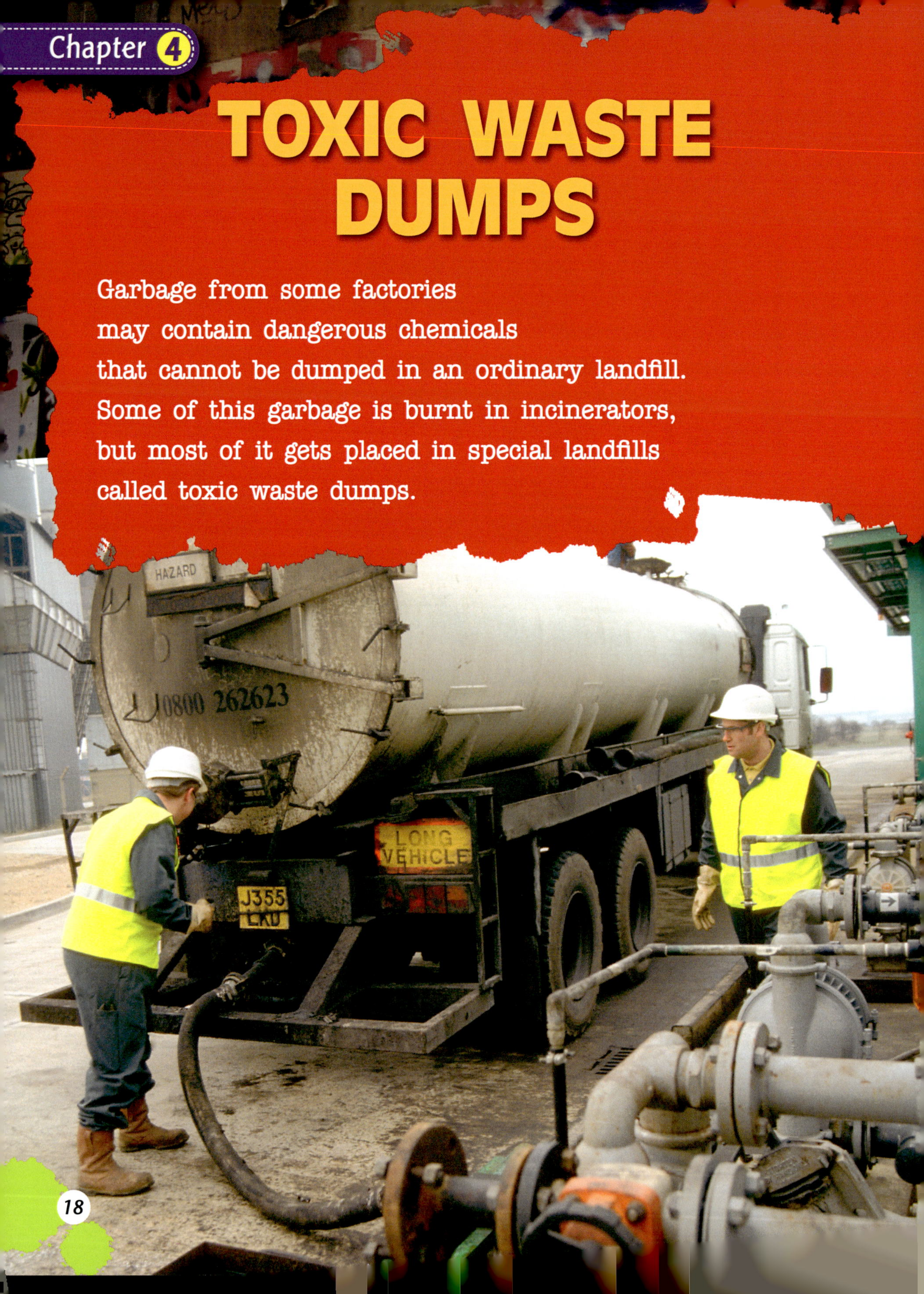

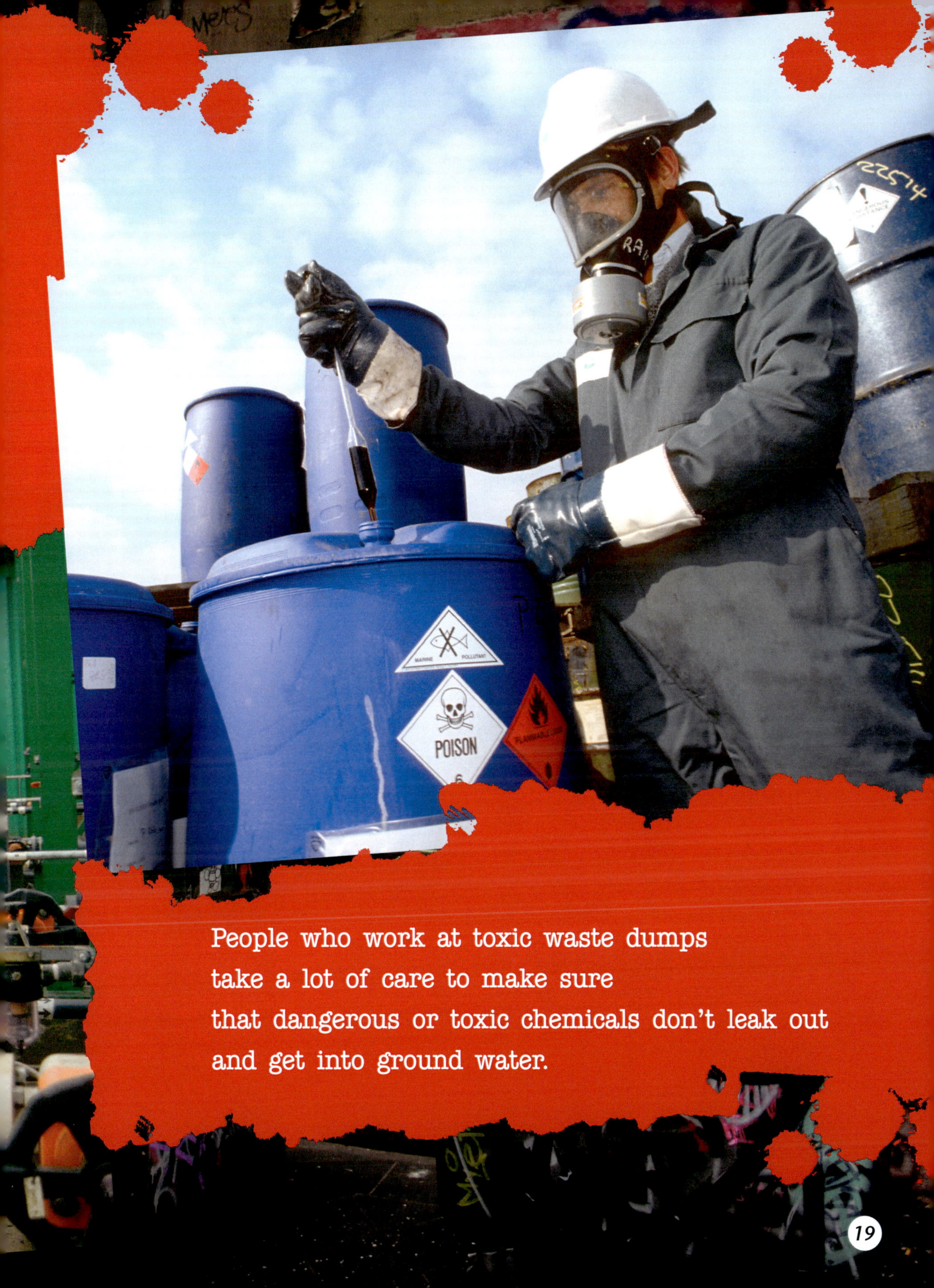

People who work at toxic waste dumps take a lot of care to make sure that dangerous or toxic chemicals don't leak out and get into ground water.

Chapter 5

THE FUTURE FOR GARBAGE

Many countries are running out of places to build new landfills.

However, there are some simple things people can do to reduce the amount of garbage they create.

For example, every day, Australians throw out over 500 000 plastic shopping bags.
If everyone took their own bags to the supermarket, it would save the cost of making all those bags, and it would stop plastic bags going into the garbage.

People can also try to buy less.
Too often, people buy more than they need.
The less people buy,
the less garbage they create.
People can also try to reuse the things they have,
instead of buying new things.

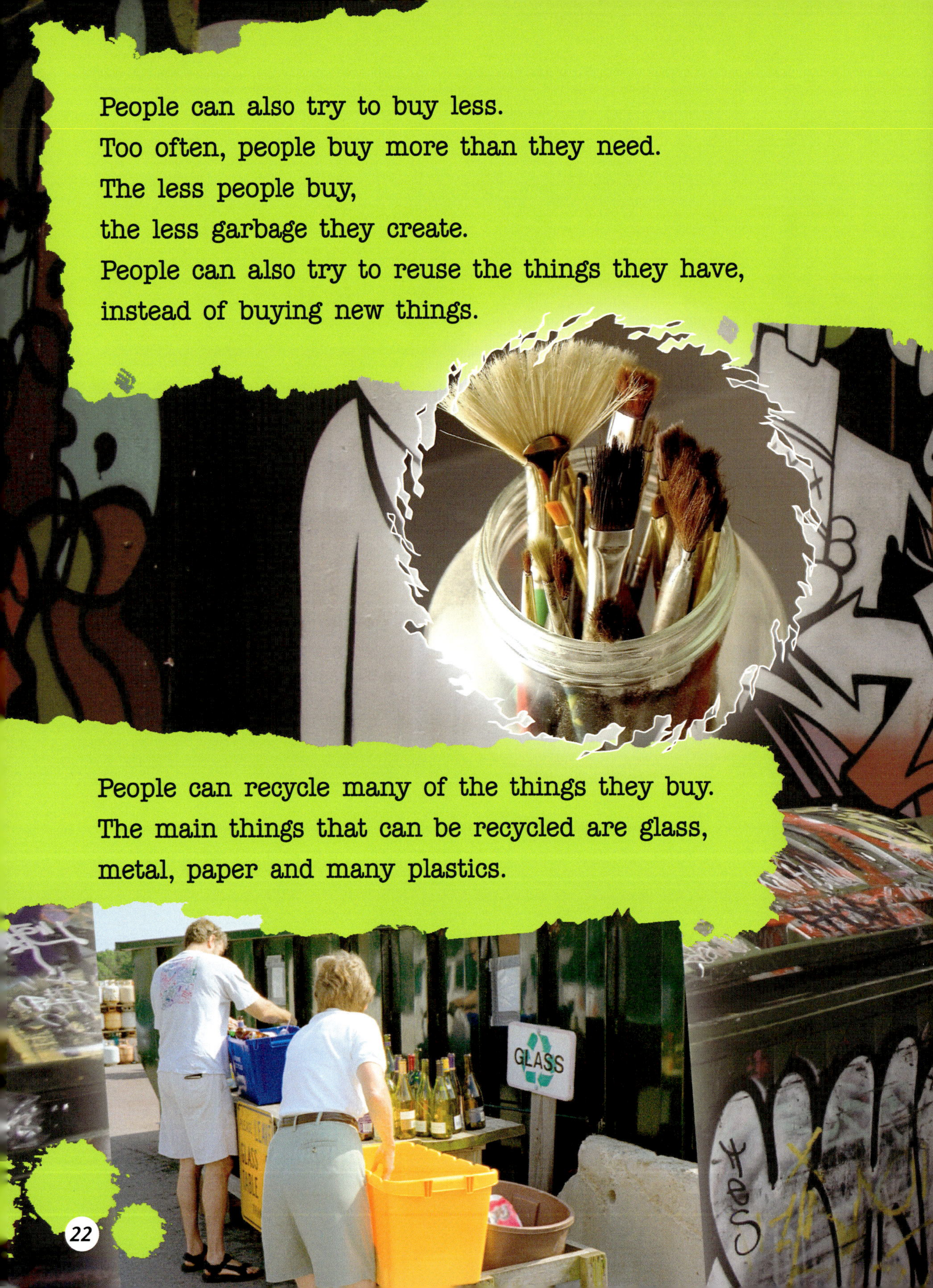

People can recycle many of the things they buy.
The main things that can be recycled are glass,
metal, paper and many plastics.

Another important thing that people can do is to turn their garden waste and food scraps into compost.

Glossary

ground water water under the ground

landfill a place set aside for dumping garbage

toxic poisonous

toxic waste dump landfill for dangerous garbage

Index